Vegetarian Cuisine

ACADEMIA BARILLA

The Taunton Press

ACADEMIA BARILLA
AMBASSADOR OF ITALIAN GASTRONOMY
THROUGHOUT THE WORLD

Academia Barilla is a global movement toward the protection, development and promotion of authentic regional Italian culture and cuisine.
With the concept of Food as Culture at our core, Academia Barilla offers a 360° view of Italy. Our comprehensive approach includes:

- a state-of-the-art culinary center in Parma, Italy;
- gourmet travel programs and hands-on cooking classes;
- the world's largest Italian gastronomic library and historic menu collection;
- a portfolio of premium artisan food products;
- global culinary certification programs;
- custom corporate services and training;
- team building activities;
- and a vast assortment of Italian cookbooks.

Thank you and we look forward to welcoming you in Italy soon!

CONTENTS

EDITED BY
ACADEMIA BARILLA

PHOTOGRAPHS
ALBERTO ROSSI

RECIPES BY
CHEF MARIO GRAZIA
CHEF LUCA ZANGA

TEXT BY
MARIAGRAZIA VILLA

ACADEMIA BARILLA EDITORIAL COORDINATION
CHATO MORANDI
ILARIA ROSSI
REBECCA PICKRELL

GRAPHIC DESIGN
PAOLA PIACCO

Besides agreeing with the aims of vegetarianism for aesthetic and moral reasons, it is my view that a vegetarian manner of living by its purely physical effect on the human temperament would most beneficially influence the lot of mankind.

ALBERT EINSTEIN

VEGETARIAN

Good news! You can choose among foods that are sustainable, healthful and light without sacrificing the pleasure of Italian cuisine. The *Bel Paese* ("beautiful country," as Italians refer to their home) has over its long history had countless luminaries inspired by a "green" way of life— from saints, poets and navigators to culinary artists. Its gastronomic culture has consistently been full of delicious vegetarian dishes. A sincere love for the fruits of the earth and for the simplicity of these ingredients are characteristic of many elegant Italian recipes.

A diet that excludes meat and fish is not simply a modern fad. It is a well-established way of life for people around the world. In Italy alone, those who professed to be vegetarian (the term derives from the Latin adjective *vegetus*, meaning healthy) are legion: from Pythagoras, with his celebrated "Pythagorean Diet," deriving from the belief in the transmigration of souls, to Empedocles of Agrigento, who preached abstinence from eating animals of the earth and sea; from the philosopher Seneca to the poet Ovid; from Tertullian, the writer, to Porphyry of Tyre, the philosopher. Although during the Middle Ages it was primarily

CUISINE

the members of monastic orders who practiced a strict vegetarian diet, in the Renaissance, there were also artists who did so, the most prominent of whom was Leonardo da Vinci.

For a person who wants to become a vegetarian, there is no need to look exclusively to the tables of the East, where many people traditionally follow a diet excluding meat or fish for religious reasons. We can observe Italian recipes dating back to ancient times that were often prepared with neither meat nor fish. In many cases, these preparations epitomize the various regional cuisines and reflect the very essence of the so-called Mediterranean diet. For example, two national stars, Spaghetti with Tomato Sauce and Pizza Margherita, are purely vegetarian.

Compared with some other green-food philosophies, that of Italian cuisine is rich in flavor without elaborate preparations or abundant spices. The key is that Italian dishes use regional ingredients of the highest quality and most dynamic flavors in ways that bring out the best in them. A simple Insalata Caprese, for example, stacks of buffalo mozzarella and tomatoes, seasoned with a drizzle of extra-virgin olive oil, a pinch of salt and a leaf of fresh basil, is an all-Italian masterpiece.

Italy has developed recipes without meat or fish that are a feast for the senses, and that contain the spirit of conviviality and emotion that any dish should possess. We are not talking about some plain little salad, but rather about truly appetizing dishes—from the typically Genovese Trenette in Pesto Sauce to Bucatini Cacio e Pepe from the cuisine of Lazio; from Parma-Style Asparagus to the Vegetable Caponata of Sicily, and to Chestnut Cake, also known as *Castagnaccio*, the traditional northern Italian torte made from chestnut flour.

As part of the Mediterranean diet, which has been "rediscovered" and nutritionally validated, we find pasta, legumes, vegetables and fruits as well as dairy products and eggs. There is fish, of course, and, even more rarely, meat. Deep within its soul, traditional Italian food is already characterized as lacto-ovo-vegetarian. And while it is an old soul, it has modern potential to grow. It is estimated that the number of people turning to a diet free from animal products will increase noticeably in the coming years, whether for health, humanitarian or ecologic reasons. Italian cuisine, already one of the most beloved in the world, may become even more so, owing to its "heart of green."

Academia Barilla, an international center dedicated to the promotion of Italian cuisine, has collected 40 vegetarian recipes from traditional Italian cuisine for this volume, divided into appetizers, first courses, main courses, side dishes and desserts. Most originate in the vast heritage of regional cuisines: Bruschetta, with extra-virgin olive oil, tomato, and basil is a great classic of the *Bel Paese*, just as are Minestrone Soup and Penne All'Arrabbiata.

Some recipes, however, are Italian because of their use of stellar local products—from Burrata cheese of Puglia to balsamic vinegar from Modena. Others are renowned for their pure creativity. With dishes such as Timbale of Venere ("Venus") Rice (with caramelized cherry tomatoes and peas); Ricotta and Olive Pesto Pastry; and the highly original Potato Sorbet, vegetarian life becomes very alluring indeed.

TOMATO-BASIL BRUSCHETTA

Preparation time: 20 minutes   Difficulty: easy

4 SERVINGS

1 **baguette** (about 400 g, or 1 lb.)
11 oz. (300 g) **tomatoes**, preferably San Marzano, or about 1 1/2 large
1 tbsp. plus 1 tsp. (20 ml) **extra-virgin olive oil**
4 **fresh basil leaves**, chopped
1 clove **garlic**
Salt to taste

Slice the baguette into pieces about 1/2 inch (1 cm) thick and toast them in the oven under the broiler for a couple of minutes on each side, or in a skillet set over medium heat.

Peel the garlic and lightly rub it over the toasted bread.

Dice the tomatoes, place them in a bowl, and season them with the oil, salt and basil.

Let tomato mixture sit for a few minutes to allow flavors to blend.

Spread tomato mixture evenly over toast and serve.

VEGETABLE CAPONATA

Preparation time: 30 minutes   Cooking time: 15 minutes   Difficulty: easy

4 SERVINGS

Scant 1/2 cup (100 ml) **extra-virgin olive oil**
1 medium **eggplant**
3 1/2 oz. (100 g) **zucchini**, *about 1/2 medium, diced*
2 oz. (50 g) **celery**, *about 2 stalks*
2 oz. (50 g) **onion**, *about 1 small*
1 oz. (25 g) **black olives**
1 oz. (20 g) **salt-packed capers**, *desalted*

2 tbsp. (15 g) **pine nuts**
2 tbsp. (15 g) **pistachio nuts**
1/2 oz. (15 g) **raisins**, *or about 1 1/2 tbsp.*
3 1/2 oz. (100 g) **crushed tomatoes**
1 bunch **basil**, *leaves torn*
1 tsp. (5 ml) **vinegar**
1 tbsp. (10 g) **sugar**
Salt and pepper *to taste*

Dice the eggplant, then put it in a colander, salt it lightly and allow it to drain for about 30 minutes. Heat two-thirds of the oil in a skillet over medium heat and fry the eggplant until tender.

With a slotted spoon, transfer eggplant to paper towels to drain.

Dice the onion and celery finely, then sauté in a skillet in the rest of the oil until they begin to brown.

Add the zucchini and sauté lightly.

Add the raisins (soak them first in lukewarm water for 15 minutes and then squeeze to remove excess water), capers, pine nuts and black olives.

Add the crushed tomatoes and the fried eggplant. Season the mixture with salt and pepper and cook for a few minutes. Add the vinegar and sugar and, lastly, the pistachios and the basil.

To serve, spread on bruschetta or a sandwich, or offer as a side dish.

CHICKPEA CAKES

Preparation time: 10 minutes   Resting time: 12 hours
Cooking time: 15 minutes   Difficulty: easy

4 SERVINGS

3 1/4 cups (300 g) **chickpea flour**
4 cups (1 l) **cold water**
2/3 cup (150 ml) **extra-virgin olive oil**
Salt and pepper *to taste*

Place chickpea flour in a large bowl and gradually add the cold water, mixing well to avoid forming lumps. Season the mixture with salt and let it rest for 12 hours. Using a skimmer, occasionally remove any foam that forms.
Heat the oven to 425°F (220°C).
Pour the oil into a shallow, wide baking pan (preferably made of tinned copper), then add the flour mixture and stir with a wooden spoon so that the oil blends uniformly (the mixture should be only 1/12 inch (about 3 mm) thick.
Bake in the oven until golden brown.
Cut the chickpea cake into small portions and sprinkle with freshly ground pepper. Serve very hot.

POTATO BASKETS AND CHIPS

Preparation time: 30 minutes   Cooking time: 3-5 minutes   Difficulty: easy

4 SERVINGS

1 lb. (400 g) **yellow potatoes**
1/2 lb. (200 g) **purple potatoes**
Vegetable oil *for frying*
Salt *to taste*

Peel the potatoes. Using a mandoline, slice the purple potatoes into thin (1/16-inch thick) rounds and let them soak in a pan of cold water.

Using the mandoline's ripple-cut blade, slice the yellow potatoes, rotating the potato 90 degrees between one cut and the next, to obtain a "waffle" design on the potato rounds.

Let them soak in cold water.

In a 4- to 5-quart heavy pot (or deep fryer) over medium heat, put 1 1/2 inches oil and heat until a deep-fat thermometer reads 350°F (175°C). Arrange some potato "waffles" into the bottom and sides of a small round fry basket to form a "basket" of potatoes.

Immerse the fry basket in the boiling oil until the potato baskets have turned golden. Drain them and transfer to paper towels. Salt lightly. Repeat until all the waffled potatoes have been fried. Next, fry the purple potato chips until crisp, 3 to 5 minutes.

Transfer them with a slotted spoon or skimmer to paper towels to drain. Set them on parchment paper and season with salt.

Fill the potato baskets with the purple potato chips and serve.

CHEESE DOUGHNUTS

Preparation time: 20 minutes   Cooking time: 20 minutes   Difficulty: medium

8 SERVINGS

4 oz. (120 g) **Pecorino cheese**
3 tbsp. (45 ml) **extra-virgin olive oil**
Vegetable oil for baking pan

FOR THE BREAD DOUGH
8 cups (1 kg) **all-purpose flour**

1 tbsp. plus 3/4 tsp. (10 g) **active dry yeast**
2 cups (630 ml) **lukewarm water**
1/2 stick (50 g) **unsalted butter**, softened
1 tbsp. plus 1 tsp. (25 g) **salt**

Make the bread dough. Put the flour onto a clean work surface and make a well in the center. Dissolve the yeast in the water. Pour the yeast into the well, and gradually incorporate it into the flour. When the dough begins to take shape, add the butter and the salt. Continue to knead until the dough is smooth and elastic.

Grate half the Pecorino and crumble the other half into pieces.

Knead the bread dough with the cheese and the oil. Form dough into a loaf, cover it with a sheet of lightly oiled plastic wrap, and let it rise in a warm place for 30 minutes to 1 hour.

Make 8 doughnuts from the dough. To make them, on a clean, lightly floured work surface, roll dough into a sausage shape, then join the ends. Arrange doughnuts on lightly oiled baking sheet, with plenty of space between, and allow to rise for another 30 minutes. Bake at 400°F (200°C) for about 20 minutes. Allow to cool before serving.

PECORINO
AND VEGETABLE STACKS

Preparation time: 30 minutes   Difficulty: medium

4 SERVINGS

*6 slices **carasau bread** or other thin, crispy flatbread*
*5 oz. (150 g) **cherry tomatoes**, thinly sliced*
*5 oz. (150 g) **shallots**, thinly sliced*
*5 oz. (150 g) **radishes**, thinly sliced*
*5 oz. (150 g) **cucumbers**, thinly sliced*
*1 oz. (30 ml) **extra-virgin olive oil***
*3 oz. (90 g) **Pecorino cheese**, shaved thin*
***Fresh chives**, chopped*
***Salt and pepper** to taste*

Soak the flatbread into a bowl of water just until it begins to soften, then cut it into 16 squares (or circles 2 to 3 inches in diameter).

Season all the vegetables with salt and pepper to taste and drizzle with a little olive oil.

Place one flatbread round in the center of a plate. Arrange tomato slices on top of the flatbread round so that they overlap slightly. Top with another flatbread round and arrange radish slices on top in the same manner. Top this with another flatbread round and a layer of cucumber slices and shallots, followed by the last flatbread round.

Scatter the shaved Pecorino on top and scattered around the stack.

Drizzle with the remaining olive oil and sprinkle with chives.

MOZZARELLA, TOMATO
AND BASIL STACKS

Preparation time: 10 minutes   Cooking time: 50 minutes   Difficulty: easy

4 SERVINGS

9 oz. (250 g) **buffalo mozzarella**
1/4 cup (60 ml) **extra-virgin olive oil**
4 large **tomatoes**
3/4 cup (15 g) **basil**, *or about 30 leaves, plus more for garnish*
Sugar, *for sprinkling*
1 clove **garlic**, *finely sliced*
1 **sprig fresh thyme**
Salt and pepper *to taste*

Heat the oven to 200°F (95°C). Slice the tomatoes and place them in a lightly oiled baking pan. Sprinkle them with the salt, a little sugar, the garlic, thyme and 1/2 tablespoon extra-virgin olive oil and bake for about 1 hour.
Wash the basil leaves and use a skimmer to dip them in boiling water. Place in an ice-water bath to cool. Transfer basil to a blender, and blend with the remaining extra-virgin olive oil until smooth.
Slice the buffalo mozzarella and season lightly with salt and pepper. Layer the mozzarella with slices of the semi-candied tomatoes.
Drizzle with extra-virgin olive oil and the basil sauce.

FAVA BEAN FRITTERS

Preparation time: 2 hours 30 minutes
Cooking time: 5 minutes   Difficulty: medium

4 SERVINGS

2 1/4 lbs. (1 kg) **dried fava beans**
1 **yellow onion**, sliced thick
2 to 3 **fennel fronds** (preferably wild fennel)
Extra-virgin olive oil
Vegetable oil for frying
Crushed red pepper flakes (optional)
Salt to taste

Soak the fava beans in water overnight. After they have soaked, drain, rinse and transfer to a pot. Cover them in fresh salted water, bring to a boil and then simmer, along with the onion slices and a few wild fennel fronds, for 2–3 hours, until the beans have softened into a purée. Run the bean purée through a sieve to extract excess liquid.
Place the purée on a marble pastry board or a clean, well-oiled work surface. Roll the mixture out into an even sheet about 1 inch (2 1/2 cm) thick. Allow to cool, then cut into strips.
In a skillet, heat 1/2 inch of oil until hot and shimmering. Fry the fritters until golden brown on all sides. With a slotted spoon, transfer fritters to a serving plate lined with paper towels to drain.
Sprinkle with salt and crushed red pepper to taste, if desired. Serve hot.

RICOTTA
AND OLIVE PESTO PASTRY

Preparation time: 30 minutes   Cooking time: 12 minutes   Difficulty: medium

4 SERVINGS

FOR THE PASTRY
1 3/4 cups plus 1 1/2 tbsp. (250 g) **all-purpose flour** or Italian "00" flour
1/3 cup (80 ml) **extra-virgin olive oil**
1/2 cup (120 ml) **water**
3/4 tsp. (5 g) **salt**

FOR THE FILLING
5 oz. (160 g) **fresh goat's-milk ricotta** or other fresh ricotta

1/2 oz. (15 g) **fresh oregano**, or about 1/2 cup
3 oz. (80 g) **black olive pesto**, about 1/3 cup
1 tbsp. plus 2 tsp. (25 ml) **extra-virgin olive oil**

FOR THE GARNISH
Mixed greens
2 tbsp. (30 ml) **extra-virgin olive oil**

Put the flour on a clean work surface and make a well in the center. Pour the oil, water, and a pinch of salt into the well, gradually incorporating them into the flour. Knead the dough until it is smooth and elastic. Wrap it in lightly oiled plastic wrap and refrigerate it for 30 minutes. Heat oven to 350°F (180°C). Using a rolling pin or pasta machine, roll out sheets of dough that are about 1/16 inch (2 mm) thick. Use a fluted pastry wheel to cut out 3-inch (8 cm) squares. Transfer dough squares to a baking sheet lined with parchment paper and bake for about 12 minutes, or until golden brown. In a bowl, whisk the ricotta together with the oil, oregano salt, pepper and olive pesto.

Fill a pastry bag with the ricotta mixture and pipe a bit of filling on a pastry square. Place another pastry square on top, like a sandwich. (You can also create stacks of 4 pastry squares.) Serve with mixed greens and a dash of olive oil.

GARGANELLI
WITH FRESH TOMATOES AND BASIL

Preparation time: 10 minutes Resting time: 2 hours
Cooking time: 9 minutes   Difficulty: easy

4 SERVINGS

12 oz. (350 g) **garganelli** *or other tube-shaped pasta*
3 1/2 tbsp. (50 ml) **extra-virgin olive oil**
1 lb. 2 oz. (500 g) **ripe tomatoes**, *about 5 medium*
10 **fresh basil leaves**
1 *clove* **garlic**, *minced*
Salt and pepper *to taste*

Halve tomatoes, remove seeds, then cut into thin strips. Place the strips in a
large salad bowl and drizzle the olive oil over the top.
Rinse the basil, gently pat dry and tear into pieces.
Sprinkle the basil and garlic over the tomato strips.
Stir carefully and let marinate in a cool place for 2 hours.
Meanwhile, bring a pot of salted water to a boil and cook the garganelli until *al
dente*. Drain, then transfer garganelli to the salad bowl with the tomatoes, garlic
and basil.
Toss gently, mixing well, before serving.

MEDITERRANEAN-STYLE
RUOTE SALAD

Preparation time: 15 minutes   Cooking time: 8 minutes   Difficulty: easy

4 SERVINGS

10 oz. (300 g) **ruote** (wagon-wheel) pasta

8 oz. (200 g) **San Marzano tomatoes**

3 oz. (80 g) **red bell pepper**, or about 1 small

3 oz. (80 g) **yellow bell pepper**, or about 1 small

3 oz. (80 g) **cucumber**, or about 1/2 cucumber

2 oz. (50 g) **celery**

2 oz. (50 g) **peas** (fresh or frozen)

31/2 oz. (100 g) **fresh fava beans**

1 1/2 oz. (40 g) **sweet red onion**, preferably Tropea, about 3/4 small

2 oz. (50 g) **black olives**, or about 1/4 cup

1 oz. (30 g) **capers**, or about 2 tbsp.

1/3 cup (80 ml) **extra-virgin olive oil**

Dried oregano (optional)

Salt to taste

Bring a large pot of salted water to a boil.

Cook the ruote in the boiling water until it is *al dente*. Rinse the pasta quickly under cold running water to stop the cooking process, then drain thoroughly. Put the pasta into a large bowl and drizzle with a little olive oil to prevent sticking.

Bring another pot of salted water to a boil. If using fresh peas, blanch them and refresh immediately in an ice-water bath. Similarly, blanch and refresh the fava beans, then peel the beans.

Rinse the olives and capers to remove their brine.

Peel the onion and peel and seed the cucumber. Cut the onion, cucumber, celery and peppers into a small dice.

Toss all the vegetables and the remaining olive oil together with the ruote. Season with a pinch of salt. Garnish with a sprinkling of oregano and a drizzle of olive oil, if desired. Serve.

This recipe is also delicious prepared with semolina gnocchi.

MACCHERONCINI
WITH SWEET RED ONION AND VEGETABLES

Preparation time: 30 minutes   Cooking time: 12 minutes   Difficulty: easy

4 SERVINGS

12 oz. (350 g) **maccheroncini** (or ziti)
1 lb. (400 g) **eggplant**, or about 1 medium
7 oz. (200 g) **red bell pepper**, or about 1 1/2 medium
7 oz. (200 g) **green bell pepper**, or about 1 1/2 medium
5 oz. (150 g) **sweet red onion**, preferably Tropea, or about 1 medium

1 1/2 oz. (40 g) **toasted slivered almonds**, or about 1/3 cup
1 1/2 oz. (40 g) **Pecorino cheese**, grated
1/3 cup plus 1 1/2 tbsp. (100 ml) **extra-virgin olive oil**
1 tbsp. (4 g) **minced parsley**
Salt and pepper to taste

Bring a large pot of salted water to a boil.
Meanwhile, combine parsley with 2 tablespoons of olive oil in a small bowl.
Peel onion and cut it into thin wedges. Dice the eggplant and peppers.
Heat 2 additional tablespoons of oil in a pan and sauté the onion over low heat.
If it starts to overcook, add a few tablespoons of water.
Separately sauté the eggplant and peppers in the remaining oil.
Mix together all the vegetables and season with salt and pepper.
Cook the maccheroncini in the pot of boiling salted water until it is *al dente*, then drain.
Combine pasta with the vegetables in a large serving bowl. Sprinkle grated Pecorino and almonds on top.

MALTAGLIATI WITH LEEK SAUCE

Preparation time: 30 minutes   Cooking time: 15 minutes   Difficulty: easy

4 SERVINGS

*14 oz. (400 g) **all-purpose flour**, or about 3 cups*
*4 large **eggs***
*4 **leeks**, white and tender green parts only*
*4 tbsp. (60 g) **unsalted butter***
*7 oz. (200 ml) **heavy cream**, at room temperature*
*2 3/4 oz. (80 g) **Parmigiano-Reggiano cheese**, grated, or about 3/4 cup plus 1 tbsp.*
***Salt** to taste*

To make the maltagliati pasta, put the flour on a clean work surface and make a well in the center. Add the eggs and knead to make a smooth, homogeneous dough. Cover the dough with a lightly oiled piece of plastic wrap and let it rest for 20 minutes.

Divide the dough into smaller pieces. Using a pasta machine set on a higher setting, for thin pasta, roll out the pieces of dough (lightly floured) to a thickness of about 0.05 inches (1.5 mm). Let pasta dry on lightly floured baking sheets for about 10 ro 15 minutes. Cut into diamond shapes, with sides approximately 1 1/3 inches (3 cm) long. (Dried lasagna noodles, broken into small pieces, can be substituted for maltagliati, if desired.)

Clean and wash the leeks and cut into thin slices.

In a large skillet over medium heat, gently fry the leeks in the butter.

Bring a large pot of salted water to a boil. Cook the pasta until it is *al dente*, then drain and add it to the pan of leeks. Add the cream, mix well, and finish with a sprinkling of grated Parmigiano-Reggiano.

Serve hot.

GENOESE SOUP

Preparation time: 1 hour   Cooking time: 30 minutes   Difficulty: easy

4 SERVINGS

3 oz. (90 g) **leeks**
2 1/2 oz. (70 g) **celery**, or about 3 stalks
1/2 lb. (200 g) **potatoes**
5 oz. (150 g) **zucchini**, or 1 small
3 oz. (80 g) **carrots**, or 2 small
4 oz. (110 g) **fennel bulb**
3 1/2 oz. (100 g) **bell pepper**, or 1 small
3 1/2 oz. (100 g) **broccoli florets**
3 1/2 oz. (100 g) **cauliflower florets**
4 **Brussels sprouts**
5 oz. (150 g) **cut spaghetti**
1/3 cup (80 ml) **extra-virgin olive oil**
5 oz. (150 g) **Parmigiano-Reggiano cheese rind**, exterior scraped clean

8 1/2 cups (2 l) **water**
Salt to taste

FOR THE PESTO
1/2 oz. (15 g) **basil leaves**, or about 3/4 cup
1/3 cup (30 g) **Parmigiano-Reggiano cheese**, grated
3 tbsp. (20 g) **aged Pecorino cheese**, grated
2 tsp. (5 g) **pine nuts**
1/2 clove **garlic**
1/3 cup plus 1 1/2 tbsp. (100 ml) **extra-virgin olive oil**
Salt to taste

Put the water in a large pot and bring it to a boil.

Meanwhile, clean and dice all the vegetables. Put the oil in another large pot over medium heat, add the vegetables, and cook for 4-5 minutes.

Pour the boiling water into the pot with the vegetables and add the Parmigiano rind. Bring to a boil, then reduce heat and simmer for at least 15 minutes. Season with salt to taste and add the pasta. Cook for 5 to 6 minutes.

Meanwhile, make the pesto. Clean the basil and lay it on paper towels to dry. In a blender, blend the basil with the oil, garlic, pine nuts and a pinch of salt. Then add the grated cheeses to the pesto and mix well. Let the soup cool and transfer it to individual bowls. Serve each portion topped with 1 tablespoon of pesto, a drizzle of cold-pressed olive oil, and a piece of Parmigiano rind.

ORECCHIETTE PUGLIESI
WITH TURNIP GREENS

Preparation time: 15 minutes   Cooking time: 12 minutes   Difficulty: easy

4 SERVINGS

10 oz. (300 g) **orecchiette**
12 oz. (350 g) **turnip greens**
4 tbsp. (60 ml) **extra-virgin olive oil**
2 **anchovy fillets**, *in oil*
1 **red chile pepper**
1 clove **garlic**, *sliced*
Salt and pepper *to taste*

Rinse the turnip greens, removing the toughest parts of the stems.
Heat 3 tablespoons of the olive oil in a shallow frying pan and sauté the garlic,
the whole chile, and the anchovy fillets. Add 3 or 4 tablespoons of water. When
the anchovies have broken down, remove the pan from the heat.
Bring a large pot of salted water to a boil. Cook the pasta, 7 to 8 minutes.
Add the turnip greens to the pasta pot and cook together until
the pasta is *al dente*.
Reheat the sauté mixture for 2 minutes before draining the pasta.
Drain the pasta and greens through a fine-mesh strainer.
Add the pasta to the anchovy sauce and mix thoroughly.
Season with freshly ground black pepper and serve immediately.

TOMATO SOUP

Preparation time: 10 minutes   Cooking time: 30 minutes   Difficulty: easy

4 SERVINGS

9 oz. (500 g) **vine-ripe tomatoes**
7 oz. (200 g) **yellow onion**
1 cup (250 ml) **water**
1 cup (20 g) **basil leaves**, torn
3 cloves **garlic**

1/2 tsp. **cayenne pepper**
1 loaf (400-500 g) **day-old baguette**, about 1 lb.
1/2 cup (100 ml) **extra-virgin olive oil**
Salt and pepper to taste

Prepare the tomatoes by making an X-shaped incision on the bottom of each tomato and blanching them in boiling water for 10 to 15 seconds. Immediately dip the tomatoes in ice water, then peel them, cut them into four sections, remove the seeds and pass the pup through a vegetable mill.

Chop the onion roughly and soften it in a saucepan in 4 tablespoons of the oil along with the whole peeled garlic cloves and the cayenne. Pour in the tomato purée and water and simmer, covered, over low heat for 25 to 30 minutes. Season with salt and pepper.

Dice the baguette and toast in a nonstick pan (without any fat) until the bread is completely dried out. Add to the soup with the basil, and continue cooking until the bread has softened and thickened the soup, 10 to 15 minutes. Remove the garlic cloves. Drizzle a little olive oil over the soup and serve.

PENNE ALL'ARRABBIATA

Preparation time: 30 minutes   Cooking time: 9 minutes   Difficulty: easy

4 SERVINGS

12 oz. (350 g) **penne**
2 tbsp. (30 ml) **extra-virgin olive oil**
18 oz. (600 g) **cherry tomatoes**, *halved (or 21 oz. whole peeled tomatoes, chopped)*
2 cloves **garlic**, *peeled and chopped*
1 tsp. **chopped parsley** *(optional)*
1 **chile pepper** *to taste (fresh or dried), or crushed red pepper flakes*
Salt *to taste*

Sauté the garlic with the olive oil and chile pepper to taste, but don't let it brown too much. If you are using a fresh chile pepper, it should be sliced, but if you are using dried hot pepper, wear disposable gloves and crush it by hand. Alternatively, you can use crushed red pepper flakes.

Once the garlic and hot pepper are slightly browned, add the tomatoes. Season with salt to taste and cook on high heat for 15 minutes, stirring occasionally.

Meanwhile, bring a large pot of salted water to a boil. Cook the penne until it is *al dente*, drain it and toss pasta with the sauce.

Garnish with chopped parsley and a few cherry tomato halves, if desired. Serve.

POTATO POLENTA

Preparation time: 15 minutes   Cooking time: 1 hour   Difficulty: easy

4–6 SERVINGS

1 1/2 cups (250 g) **cornmeal**
1 lb. (500 g) **potatoes**
2 1/2 tbsp. (35 g) **unsalted butter**
6 1/3 cups (1 1/2 l) **water**
Salt *to taste*

Wash and peel the potatoes and cut into cubes.
Bring the water to a boil with the butter, then add salt and cook the potatoes.
After about 15 minutes, whisk in the cornmeal. Cook over low heat, stirring
constantly with a wooden spoon, for about 40 minutes.
Serve immediately, topped with cheese, such as Parmigiano-Reggiano or
Pecorino, if desired.
Any leftover polenta can be sliced and reheated in the oven, on the grill or in a
skillet.

SPACCATELLE
WITH VEGETABLE RAGOUT

Preparation time: 40 minutes   Cooking time: 9 minutes   Difficulty: medium

4 SERVINGS

10 oz. (300 g) **spaccatelle** *(or other short tube pasta, such as tortiglioni)*
7 oz. (200 g) **tomatoes**, *about 2 medium*
3 1/2 oz. (100 g) **eggplant**
5 oz. (150 g) **zucchini**, *or 1 small*
5 oz. (150 g) **red bell pepper**, *or 1 small*
5 oz. (150 g) **yellow bell pepper**, *or 1 small*
31/2 oz. (100 g) **carrots**

2 oz. (50 g) **leeks**, *white part only, about 1/3 leek*
2 oz. (50 g) **celery**, *about 2 stalks*
1 1/4 oz. (35 g) **shallots**
3 1/2 tbsp. (50 ml) **extra-virgin olive oil**
4 or 5 **basil leaves**, *coarsely chopped*
Salt to taste

Dice the eggplant, then place in a colander, salt lightly and allow it to drain for about 30 minutes. Dice the carrots, celery, bell peppers and zucchini. Peel and dice the shallots. Slice the white part of the leek. Heat the oil in a pan and sauté leeks with the celery and carrots. Add the rest of the vegetables (except the tomatoes), beginning with the eggplant, then adding the peppers, shallots, and zucchini. Add salt to taste.

Peel and dice the tomatoes, remove the seeds and add to the sauté mix to form a ragout.

Continue cooking for a few more minutes. Add the basil.

Bring a large pot of salted water to a boil. Cook the pasta until it is *al dente*, then drain it.

In a serving dish, pour the ragout over the pasta, toss to coat, and serve.

SPAGHETTI
WITH TOMATO SAUCE

Preparation time: 30 minutes   Cooking time: 8 minutes   Difficulty: easy

4 SERVINGS

12 oz. (350 g) **spaghetti**
2 tbsp. (30 ml) **extra-virgin olive oil**
1 1/3 lbs. (600 g) or 2 1/2 cups **peeled tomatoes**, *chopped, or tomato purée*
3 1/2 oz. (100 g) **onion**, *chopped*
1 clove **garlic**
8 **basil leaves**, *chopped*
1 1/2 oz. (40 g) **Parmigiano-Reggiano cheese**, *grated*
Salt and pepper *to taste*

Sauté the onion in the oil in a saucepan, together with the clove of garlic. When the onion turns golden brown, add the chopped tomatoes or the tomato purée and lastly, add salt and pepper. Cook the sauce over high heat for about 20 minutes, stirring from time to time. Then remove the garlic and add the basil. Bring a large pot of salted water to a boil. Cook the spaghetti until *al dente*, drain and add the tomato sauce.
Sprinkle with the grated Parmigiano-Reggiano.

TIMBALE OF VENERE ("VENUS") RICE

Preparation time: 1 hour 10 minutes
Cooking time: 2 hours   Difficulty: medium

4 SERVINGS

2/3 cup (120 g) **black Venere rice**
3 1/2 tbsp. (50 ml) **extra-virgin olive oil**
3 1/2 tsp. (15 g) **sugar**
7 oz. (200 g) **cherry tomatoes**,
preferably Pachino, plus more for garnish
1 clove **garlic**, *thinly sliced*

3 to 4 **basil leaves**
Dried oregano
1/3 cup (50 g) **peas**
Salt and pepper *to taste*
Parsley, *for garnish (optional)*

Heat the oven to 200°F (95°C).

Halve the tomatoes, season with salt and place in a baking pan. Sprinkle the sliced garlic, a pinch of oregano and 1 tablespoon (15 ml) of the olive oil on the tomato halves and bake for about 1 hour.

In the meantime, bring about 1 1/4 cups of salted water to a boil in a saucepan, add the Venere rice and cook until *al dente*, 25 to 30 minutes, then drain any excess water. In another pan of salted boiling water, cook the peas for 2 minutes. Drain and refresh in an ice-water bath.

In a bowl, mix together the rice, peas, and cherry tomatoes.

Wash and dry the basil, tear into pieces, then sprinkle on top of the tomatoes, along with half the remaining olive oil. Season with salt and pepper.

Oil four individual ramekins. Spoon the rice mixture into ramekins. Place ramekins in a roasting pan, and add enough hot water to the pan so that it reaches halfway up ramekins. Place in a 350°F (180°C) oven until the rice is hot again, about 15 minutes.

Invert ramekins onto individual plates and drizzle with olive oil. Garnish each timbale with a sprig of parsley, if desired.

POTATOES AU GRATIN

Preparation time: 20 minutes   Cooking time: 35-40 minutes   Difficulty: easy

4 SERVINGS

1 lb. (400 g) **potatoes**
7 oz. (200 ml) **heavy cream**
2/3 cup (150 ml) **milk**
Unsalted butter *for pan*
1 clove **garlic**
Salt and white pepper *to taste*

Heat an oven to 350°F (180°C).
Peel and wash the potatoes. Slice the potatoes very thin using
a mandoline or slicer.
Pour the cream into a saucepan and add the milk, potatoes, salt,
pepper and whole clove of garlic.
Cook over moderate heat, covered, until the potatoes are tender.
Remove the garlic.
Butter a baking dish and arrange the potatoes evenly across
the bottom, in layers.
Bake at 350°F (180°C) for about 20 minutes, until the surface of the potatoes
begins to brown. Let the potatoes cool before cutting into serving portions.
Before serving, reheat in the oven at 350°F (180°C) for several minutes.

TRENETTE IN PESTO SAUCE

Preparation time: 20 minutes   Cooking time: 12 minutes   Difficulty: easy

4 SERVINGS

12 oz. (350 g) **trenette pasta** *or linguine fini*
1 oz. (30 g) **basil leaves**, *or about 1 1/2 cups*
1/2 oz. (15 g) **pine nuts**, *about 2 tbsp.*
2 oz. (60 g) **Parmigiano-Reggiano cheese**, *grated, or about 2/3 cup*
1 1/2 oz. (40 g) **aged Pecorino cheese**, *grated, or about 1/3 cup plus 1 tbsp.*
1 clove **garlic**
7 oz. (200 g) **potatoes**, *or about 1 1/2 medium, diced*
3 1/2 oz. (100 g) **green beans**
7 oz. (200 ml) **extra-virgin olive oil**
Salt *to taste*

Rinse the basil, then gently dry it in a dish towel. In a mortar, pound the basil,
pine nuts, garlic, olive oil, a pinch of salt, and the grated cheeses. Alternatively,
blend the ingredients in a blender, using the pulse function to avoid overheating
the pesto. Pour it into a bowl and cover with olive oil.
In a pan of salted water, boil the potatoes and the chopped green beans. After 5
minutes, add the trenette to the same pot to cook until *al dente*. Drain,
reserving some of the cooking water.
Transfer trenette and vegetables to a large bowl, add the pesto and mix well,
diluting the mixture with a bit of cooking water and a drizzle of olive oil.

PARMA-STYLE ASPARAGUS

Preparation time: 15 minutes   Cooking time: 10 minutes   Difficulty: easy

4 SERVINGS

1 3/4 lbs. (800 g) **asparagus**
4 tbsp. (60 g) **unsalted butter**
2 oz. (50 g) **Parmigiano-Reggiano cheese**, *grated, or about 1/2 cup*
Salt *to taste*

Wash the asparagus. Remove the hard ends and cut all the stalks to the same length. Tie them into small bundles and stand them upright in a saucepan of salted water. Boil them, tips upward, to the point that they are still firm (about 10 minutes). Drain and arrange on a serving dish.

Sprinkle the asparagus tips with the grated Parmigiano-Reggiano.

Meanwhile, melt the butter in a saucepan. When it is frothy, pour it over the asparagus.

EGGPLANT SALAD
WITH FENNEL, OLIVES AND RAISINS

Preparation time: 30 minutes   Cooking time: 20 minutes   Difficulty: easy

4 SERVINGS

1 lb. (500 g) **eggplant**
8 oz. (200 g) **red onions**, *or about 1 1/2 medium*
14 oz. (400 g) **red bell peppers**, *or about 2 medium*
12 oz. (300 g) **tomatoes**, *or about 3 medium*
3 1/2 oz. (100 g) **black olives**, *pitted*
3 1/2 oz. (100 g) **raisins**, *about 2/3 cup packed*

1 oz. (30 g) **pine nuts**, *or about 3 1/2 tbsp.*
1 **fennel bulb**
1 tsp. **sugar**
1/3 cup (80 ml) **red wine vinegar**
1/3 cup (80 ml) **extra-virgin olive oil**
2 cloves **garlic**
1/2 oz. (15 g) **fresh basil leaves**, *or about 3/4 cup*
Salt and pepper *to taste*

Dice the eggplant, then put it in a colander, salt it lightly and allow it to drain for about 30 minutes.

Soak the raisins in warm water for 15 minutes, then drain and squeeze out any excess liquid.

Dice the onion, peppers, fennel bulb, garlic and tomatoes. Heat the oil in a pan over medium heat and sauté the onion.

Add the eggplant, peppers, fennel and garlic. Let them cook until the eggplant softens, about 10 minutes. Add the olives and raisins, and, lastly, the tomatoes.

Season the vegetables with basil, a handful of salt and a generous grind of pepper. Cover the pan and let the liquid reduce for 5 minutes, stirring occasionally. Add the sugar and vinegar and let it continue cooking, uncovered, until the mixture is dense and the vegetables are tender.

In a heated nonstick pan, lightly toast the pine nuts. Garnish the mixture with basil, chopped fennel fronds, and toasted pine nuts and serve.

PUMPKIN PURÉE
WITH GOAT CHEESE

Preparation time: 20 minutes   Cooking time: 1 hour   Difficulty: easy

4 SERVINGS

2 1/4 lb. (1 kg) **pumpkin** (or 1 lb./450 g
canned packed pumpkin)
12 oz. (350 g) **goat cheese**, fresh
1/2 cup (120 ml) **heavy cream**
2 sprigs **rosemary**
Nutmeg to taste

4 **sprigs chives**
Extra-virgin olive oil to taste
Balsamic vinegar, preferably of
Modena, to taste
Salt and pepper to taste

Heat oven to 320°F (160°C). Cut the pumpkin into eight sections and scoop out and discard seeds. Sprinkle rosemary, a drizzle of olive oil and a pinch of salt to pumpkin flesh. On a lightly greased baking sheet, place the pumpkin sections cut side down and bake for about 1 hour. (For an optional garnish of pumpkin chips, use a mandoline to slice one of the sections very thin and then fry in vegetable oil until crispy.)

Meanwhile, purée the goat cheese with the cream, a little olive oil, salt and freshly ground black pepper in a blender then refrigerate.

Chop the chives and set aside. When pumpkin is cooked, let it cool. Scrape out the flesh. Add nutmeg, a little olive oil and salt and pepper to taste.

Mix well with a fork or pass mixture through a sieve until smooth. Use a pasta or cake mold to shape the purée on a serving plate. Place two scoops of goat cheese mousse on top. Garnish with pumpkin chips (if desired), plus chives, a dash of balsamic vinegar and freshly ground pepper to taste.

RECCO-STYLE FOCACCIA

Preparation time: 30 minutes Rising time: 1 hour
Cooking time: 6-8 minutes   Difficulty: easy

4 SERVINGS

*4 cups (500 g) **all-purpose flour** or Italian "00" flour*
*1 1/4 cups (300 ml) **cold water***
*1 lb. (500 g) **Crescenza or Taleggio cheese**, diced*
*1/3 cup plus 1 1/2 tbsp. (100 ml) **extra-virgin olive oil***
***Salt** to taste*

Place the flour on a clean work surface and make a well in the center. Pour 3 tbsp. of the oil into the well and incorporate it into the flour, gradually adding the cold water and kneading until the dough is very soft. Form dough into a ball. Place dough in a bowl, cover it with a cloth and let it rest at room temperature for 1 hour. Heat oven to 500° F (260°C).
Knead the dough for a few minutes, divide it, and let it rest for 5 minutes. Roll out one piece so that it is very thin, about 1/12 inch (3 mm) thick. Use your fists to spread the dough until it is almost transparent.
Place the dough on a greased baking sheet and cover it with the cheese. Roll out the second piece of dough as you did the first. Place it over cheese and press down around the cheese, creating dimples 1/3-1/2 inch (1 cm) in diameter. Sprinkle with salt and drizzle with remaining oil. Spread the oil over the surface, pressing down on cheese pieces.
Bake focaccia for 6 to 8 minutes, or until the surface is golden brown. Cut it into large portions and serve immediately.

POTATO AND CHEESE PANCAKES

Preparation time: 30 minutes   Cooking time: 10 minutes   Difficulty: easy

4 SERVINGS

1/2 lb. (200 g) **Montasio or Asiago cheese**, *large diced*
2/3 lb. (300 g) **potatoes**
1 1/2 tbsp. (20 g) **unsalted butter**
3 tsp. (20 g) **salt**

Scrub the potatoes and cook them, skins on, in a pot of boiling salted water until they are tender but still firm, about 15 minutes. Let them cool, then peel them and grate them using the coarse-grating surface of a box grater.
Melt the butter in a skillet, add the potatoes, and brown them, seasoning with a pinch of salt. Add the cheese and mix together. Let the potato-cheese mixture brown like a pancake. After about 5 minutes, flip it and brown the other side for 5 minutes. Serve immediately.

EGGPLANT STUFFED
WITH GOAT CHEESE

Preparation time: 40 minutes   Cooking time: 5 minutes   Difficulty: medium

4 SERVINGS

1 3/4 lbs. (800 g) **eggplant**
3/4 lb. (350 g) **sweet red onions**,
preferably Tropea, sliced
1 lb. (400 g) **tomatoes**, or about 4
medium
11 oz. (300 g) **soft goat cheese**,
preferably caprino

1 cup (250 ml) **white vinegar**
2 1/2 tbsp. (30 g) **sugar**
1 **bunch chives**, sliced thin, plus more
for wrapping
6 large **basil leaves**
2/3 cup (150 ml) **extra-virgin olive oil**
Salt and pepper to taste

Slice eggplant lengthwise, then put it in a colander, salt it lightly and allow it to
drain for about 30 minutes.

In a nonstick pan over medium heat, sauté eggplant with a little oil. When
tender, place eggplant on paper towels to drain. Mix the goat cheese with the
sliced chives and season with salt and pepper to taste. In a blender, purée the
tomatoes with about 2 tablespoons (30 ml) of olive oil. Strain the purée
in a fine-mesh sieve and season with salt and pepper.

Place onions in a pan with the sugar and vinegar and bring liquid to a boil.
Remove from heat and strain.

Purée the basil leaves with 2 tablespoons (30 ml) of olive oil.

Place a tablespoon of cheese in the middle of each eggplant slice and roll it up.
Tie whole chives around rolls so they stay closed. Arrange them on serving
plates with a spoonful of sweet-and-sour onions, a spoonful of tomato sauce and
a drizzle of basil oil.

VEGETABLE STACKS

Preparation time: 40 minutes   Cooking time: 5 minutes   Difficulty: easy

4 SERVINGS

10 oz. (300 g) **tomatoes** *for slicing, or about 2 large*
7 oz. (200 g) **yellow bell peppers**, *or about 2 medium*
5 oz. (150 g) **celeriac** *(or Jerusalem artichoke)*
7 oz. (200 g) **yellow squash**
5 oz. (150 g) **radicchio**
7 oz. (200 g) **fennel bulb**
9 oz. (250 g) **zucchini**

6 small **eggplants**
7 oz. (200 g) **red onions**
7 oz. (200 g) **leeks**, *white parts only*
1/3 cup (100 ml) **milk**
3 1/2 tbsp. (50 ml) **extra-virgin olive oil**
Flour
Juice from 1 **lemon**
Vegetable oil *for frying, as needed*
Salt and pepper *to taste*

Cut the white parts of the leeks into thin strips. Soak for 10 minutes in the milk, then drain. Coat in flour. Heat oil in a pan until shimmering and deep-fry leeks. Drain on a paper towel, season with salt, and set aside.

Roast or grill the peppers, then peel them and slice them crosswise into rounds. Slice the eggplant, onion, and zucchini into rounds of about 1/8-inch (3 mm) thick. Slice the celeriac and squash 1/8-inch (3 mm) thick, then cut them into rounds. Slice the tomatoes, fennel and radicchio.

Put a few drops of lemon juice into a pot of boiling salted water, and cook the celeriac for 5 minutes.

Heat the oven to 475°F (245°C). Drizzle the eggplant, onion, zucchini, celeriac, squash, fennel, and radicchio with olive oil and roast in a roasting pan for about 35 minutes. (Grilling the vegetables is an option). Place all the cooked vegetables in a bowl, season with salt and pepper and a drizzle of oil and let marinate for at least 15 minutes. Layer vegetables to create stacks. Garnish with the deep-fried leeks.

GRILLED VEGETABLE MEDLEY

Preparation time: 1 1/2 hours   Cooking time: 20 minutes   Difficulty: easy

4 SERVINGS

8 oz. (250 g) **eggplant**
7 oz. (200 g) **zucchini**, or 1 medium
7 oz. (200 g) **yellow bell pepper**, or
about 2 medium
7 oz. (200 g) **red bell pepper**, or about
2 medium
6 oz. (160 g) **carrots**, peeled
5 oz. (150 g) **sweet red onions**,
preferably Tropea, or about 1 medium

4 oz. (120 g) **vine-ripened tomato**, or
about 1 medium
3 1/2 oz. (100 g) **Pecorino cheese**,
preferably Tuscan
3 1/2 tbsp. (50 ml) **extra-virgin olive
oil**, preferably Tuscan
Fresh basil leaves to taste
Salt to taste

Slice the eggplant, carrots, onion and zucchini.
Cut the tomato into wedges. Grill the sliced vegetables and whole peppers. Peel
the peppers and cut lengthwise into strips. Place all the vegetables in a bowl
and toss gently with the olive oil, a pinch of salt and hand-torn basil leaves. Let
vegetables marinate for at least 1 hour. Grate or thinly shave the Pecorino.
Arrange the vegetables on a serving plate topped with the cheese. Drizzle with
olive oil and garnish with fresh basil leaves, if desired.

ROASTED POTATOES
WITH TOMATOES AND ONIONS

Preparation time: 20 minutes   Cooking time: 20 minutes   Difficulty: easy

4 SERVINGS

*1 1/3 lbs. (600 g) **potatoes**, or about 3 medium*
*11 oz. (300 g) **yellow onions**, or about 2 medium*
*1 lb. (400 g) **tomatoes**, or about 4 medium*
*3 tbsp. (40 ml) **extra-virgin olive oil***
*1 1/2 oz. (40 g) **Pecorino cheese**, grated, or about 1/3 cup plus 1 tbsp.*
***Salt and pepper** to taste*

Scrub and peel the potatoes. Cut them into rounds about 1/8 inch (3 mm)
thick and place them in a bowl of cold water.
Slice the tomatoes into rounds about 1/4 inch (5 mm) thick.
Peel the onions and slice them into rings 1/10 inch (2 mm) thick.
Heat the oven to 350°F (180°C). Cut a piece of parchment large enough to cover
the bottom of a baking pan. Arrange the potatoes, tomatoes, and onions on the
parchment, alternating them until all the ingredients have been used.
Season with salt and pepper.
Finish with a drizzle of olive oil and a sprinkling of Pecorino cheese.
Bake for about 20 minutes. Cover with aluminum foil if the vegetables become
too dry.

GRATIN OF CAULIFLOWER, BRUSSELS SPROUTS AND LEEKS

Preparation time: 30 minutes   Cooking time: 20 minutes   Difficulty: easy

4 SERVINGS

FOR THE VEGETABLES
5 oz. (150 g) **cauliflower florets**
5 oz. (150 g) **leeks**
5 oz. (150 g) **Brussels sprouts**

FOR THE BÉCHAMEL
4 tbsp. (60 g) **unsalted butter**, plus
more for drizzling

1/3 cup (40 g) **all-purpose flour**
2 cups (1/2 l) **milk**
1 3/4 oz. (50 g) **Parmigiano-Reggiano
cheese**, grated, or about 1/2 cup
Nutmeg to taste
Salt to taste

Rinse the cauliflower, leeks and Brussels sprouts. Remove and discard the roots and green parts of the leeks and the wilted outer leaves of the Brussels sprouts. Boil the vegetables separately in salted water until they can be easily pierced with a knife. Drain and let them cool.

Prepare the béchamel. In a small saucepan, melt 3 tablespoons (45 g) of the butter and stir in the flour to create a roux. Cook for 1 to 2 minutes over low heat, until the mixture turns yellow.

Boil the milk, add it to the roux, and return to a boil for one minute. Season with salt and a grating of nutmeg.

Heat oven to 350°F (180 °C). Grease four ramekins (or a single baking dish, especially for leeks) with the remaining butter. Place the vegetables (together or separate, as you desire) in the baking dishes and pour béchamel over them.

Sprinkle them with Parmigiano-Reggiano and a little melted butter.

Roast the vegetables for 20 minutes or until a golden crust forms.

CHESTNUT CAKE

Preparation time: 15 minutes   Cooking time: 30 minutes   Difficulty: easy

4 SERVINGS

1 2/3 cups (200 g) **chestnut flour**
2/3 cup (140 ml) **water**
2 oz. (55 g) **raisins**, *or about 1/3 cup*
1/2 oz. (15 g) **pine nuts**, *or about 2 tbsp.*
Fennel seeds *to taste*
1 tbsp. (15 ml) **extra-virgin olive oil**
Salt *to taste*

Soak the raisins in hot water for about 15 minutes, then drain, squeeze out excess water, and dry them.
Put the chestnut flour in a bowl together with a generous pinch of salt. Pour in the water in a thin steady stream, whisking until you obtain a smooth batter. Heat the oven to 350°F (180°C).
Lightly oil a baking pan and pour in the batter. Sprinkle the batter with the raisins, the pine nuts and a pinch of fennel seeds. Pour the remaining oil in a thin steady stream over the batter.
Bake for about 30 minutes and let cool before serving.

CHOCOLATE-COATED FIGS

Preparation time: 20 minutes   Cooking time: 5 minutes   Difficulty: easy

4 SERVINGS

1 3/4 lb. (800 g) **dried figs**
5 oz. (150 g) **almonds**
2 **cloves**, *crushed*
2 1/2. oz. (70 g) **candied citrus peel**, *chopped*
1 **pinch cinnamon**
3 1/2 oz. (100 g) **dark chocolate**, *grated*
2 2/3 oz. (75 g) **sugar**, *or about 1/4 cup plus 2 tbsp*

Toast the almonds in a small dry skillet over medium-high heat until fragrant, 3 to 5 minutes, stirring frequently. Set aside to cool, then chop almonds and mix them with the citrus peel and cloves.

In a bowl, mix the sugar, cinnamon and grated chocolate.

Heat the oven to 350°F (180°C). Remove stems from figs. Cut figs open from top, leaving them whole, then fill with a bit of the almond mixture. Close figs firmly and place on a baking sheet.

Bake figs until they begin to brown. Remove them from the oven and, while they are still hot, roll them in the chocolate mixture. (Alternatively, you can melt the chocolate and dip the hot figs in the chocolate mixed with a little water and a pinch of cinnamon.)

Store chocolate-coated figs in tins lined with wax paper.

CHOCOLATE FONDUE

Preparation time: 15 minutes   Difficulty: easy

4 SERVINGS

FOR THE FONDUE
1 lb. 5 oz. (600 g) **dark chocolate**,
finely chopped
Extra-virgin olive oil, *as needed*

FOR THE FRUIT
2 **bananas**
10 oz. (300 g) **strawberries**
2 **kiwifruit**

Melt the chocolate in a saucepan over low heat. Dilute with a few drops of extra-virgin olive oil until you have the desired density. Transfer to a fondue pot set over a candle flame or to a small warmed bowl.
Wash the strawberries. Peel the bananas and the kiwifruit.
Cut the fruit into pieces and thread them onto wooden skewers. Dip skewers in the chocolate fondue.

SUMMER FRUIT SALAD

Preparation time: 15 minutes   *Difficulty: easy*

4 SERVINGS

2 **melons**, *such as cantaloupe or honeydew*
3 1/2 oz. (100 g) **raspberries**
1/2 cup (100 ml) **brandy** *(or passito sweet wine)*

Rinse and dry the melons. Cut them in half and remove all the seeds.
Using a melon baller, scoop out the flesh in small balls, taking care not to
damage the skin. The shells will be used to serve the fruit salad in.
Place the raspberries in a colander; rinse and dry them gently.
Place the melon balls and raspberries in a bowl and give fruit a healthy
splash of brandy or passito.
Fill the melon shells with the fruit salad. Refrigerate for 30 minutes
before serving.

BAKED APPLES

Preparation time: 20 minutes   Cooking time: 30 minutes   Difficulty: easy

4 SERVINGS

4 **apples***, such as Reinette or Golden Delicious*
3 oz. (80 g) **apricot preserves***, or about 1/4 cup*
1 1/2 oz. (40 g) **raisins***, or about 1/4 cup packed*
1 1/2 oz. (40 g) **slivered almonds***, or about 1/3 cup, plus more for serving, if desired*
2 tbsp. (25 g) **brown sugar**
Confectioners' sugar*, for dusting (optional)*

Heat the oven to 325°F (160°C). Core apples with corer. Stand apples up and make 4 evenly spaced vertical cuts starting from top of each apple and stopping halfway from bottom to keep apple intact.

In a well-heated nonstick pan, toss the almonds for a few seconds to toast them on both sides.

Combine the raisins and preserves in a bowl. Pack the center of each apple with the mixture. Sprinkle brown sugar on top.

Arrange the apples in a baking dish, sprinkle the toasted almonds on top and bake for about 15 minutes, or until apples are very tender but still intact. Serve dusted with confectioners' sugar and more toasted almonds, if desired.

POTATO SORBET

Preparation time: 20 minutes   Maturation: 6 hours   Difficulty: easy

4 SERVINGS

1 lb. (500 g) **potatoes** *(yellow, white or purple)*
2 cups (500 ml) **water**
2 oz. (60 g) **powdered dextrose**
1/2 lb. (250 g) **sugar**
1 1/2 tsp. (10 g) **sorbet stabilizer** *(available online at pastrychef.com)*

When choosing a potato, remember that the color and aroma of the sorbet will reflect the type of potato used.
Cook the potatoes in a pot of boiling water until tender. Pass the boiled potatoes through a potato ricer.
In a bowl, mix the sugar with the dextrose and stabilizer. Heat the water to 150°F (65°C) and pour it into the sugar mixture, whisking as you pour. Blend in the potatoes and quickly cool the mixture to 40°F (4°C) by placing the bowl in an ice-water bath.
Refrigerate the mixture until completely cooled, about 6 hours, then freeze the sorbet in your ice cream maker according to the manufacturer's instructions.

CITRUS FRUIT SOUP

Preparation time: 30 minutes   Difficulty: easy

4 SERVINGS

2 *oranges*
1 *yellow grapefruit*
1 *pink grapefruit*
2 *mandarin oranges*
1 oz. (30 g) *shelled pistachios*, or about 1/4 cup
2 tbsp. (25 g) *sugar*

Use a vegetable peeler to zest 1 orange, half a yellow grapefruit and half a pink grapefruit, making sure not to include the bitter white pith.

Slice the peels into thin strips. Put the peels in a small pot of water over medium-high heat. As soon as the water comes to a boil, drain the peels, add cold water to the pan and repeat the process two more times.

Remove the peel and pith from the remainder of the fruit. Working over a bowl to catch the juices, use a paring knife to slice between the sections and membranes of each fruit; remove the segments whole, reserving the fruit and juice, and transfer them to the refrigerator.

Strain the boiled peels and put the pot back on the heat, adding the sugar and a few tablespoons of the reserved citrus juice.

Bring mixture to a boil, then turn off the heat and let it cool. In another pot, blanch the pistachios for 30 seconds so they will be easier to peel. After peeling, finely chop the nuts.

Divide the fruit, fruit juice and syrup evenly among serving bowls. Garnish the soup with peels and pistachios.

INGREDIENTS INDEX

PHOTO CREDITS

All photographs are by ACADEMIA BARILLA except the following:
pages 6, 95 ©123RF

The Taunton Press
Inspiration for hands-on living®

The Taunton Press, Inc.
63 South Main Street
PO Box 5506, Newtown, CT 06470-5506
e-mail: tp@taunton.com

Translations:
Catherine Howard - Mary Doyle - John Venerella - Free z'be, Paris
Salvatore Ciolfi - Rosetta Translations SARL - Rosetta Translations SARL

LIBRARY OF CONGRESS CATALOGING-IN-PUBLICATION DATA IN PROGRESS
ISBN: 978-1-62710-047-2

Printed in China
10 9 8 7 6 5 4 3 2 1